WHO WAS...?

Henry VIII

Kay Barnham

First published in 2007 by Wayland
Copyright © Wayland 2007

Wayland
338 Euston Road
London NW1 3BH

Wayland Australia
Level 17/207 Kent Street
Sydney, NSW 2000

Editor: Victoria Brooker
Designer: Jane Stanley

Barnham, Kay
  Who was Henry VIII?
  1. Henry, VIII, King of England, 1491-1547 - Juvenile
  literature 2. Great Britain - Kings and rulers - Biography
  - Juvenile literature 3. Great Britain - History - Henry
  VIII, 1509-1547 - Juvenile literature
  I. Title
  942'.052'092
ISBN 978 0 7502 5196 9
Printed in China
Wayland is a division of Hachette Children's Books, an Hachette Livre UK Company.

For permission to reproduce the following pictures, the author and publisher would like to thank: ©The Board of Trustees of the Armouries/Heritage-Images: 7, ©The Berger Collection at the Denver Art Museum, USA/Bridgeman Art Library, London: 6, ©David Crausby/Alamy Images: 17, © Gianni Dagli Orti/Corbis: 18, Cover Getty Images (Hulton Archive): 12, ©Hardwick Hall, Derbyshire, UK/National Trust Photographic Library/P.A. Burton/Bridgeman Art Library: 21, ©Hatfield House, Hertfordshire, UK/Bridgeman Art Library, London: 5, ©Hever Castle, Kent, UK/Bridgeman Art Library, London: 11, ©Kunsthistorisches Museum, Vienna, Austria/Bridgeman Art Library, London: 14, ©Mary Rose Trust: 1, 9, ©Francis G. Mayer/Corbis: 4, 16, ©Musee des Arts Decoratifs, Paris, France/Giraudon/Bridgeman/Art Library, London: 10, ©Private Collection/Bridgeman Art Library, London: 13, ©Private Collection/© Philip Mould Ltd, London/Bridgeman Art Library, London 8, 20, ©Private Collection/The Stapleton Collection/Bridgeman Art Library, London: 15 Topham Picturepoint, TopFoto.co.uk: 19

Contents

Words in **bold** can be found in the glossary.

Who was Henry VIII?

Henry VIII ruled over England and Ireland from 1509 to 1547. He was a very powerful king. Henry VIII is famous for having six wives and for arguing with the **Roman Catholic Church**.

This picture is of Henry VIII. He was the second Tudor **monarch**. His father, Henry VII, was the first.

Henry VIII belonged to the Tudor family. Tudor monarchs ruled England from 1485 to 1603.

IT'S TRUE!

Henry VIII loved music. He had 58 musicians at his royal **court**.

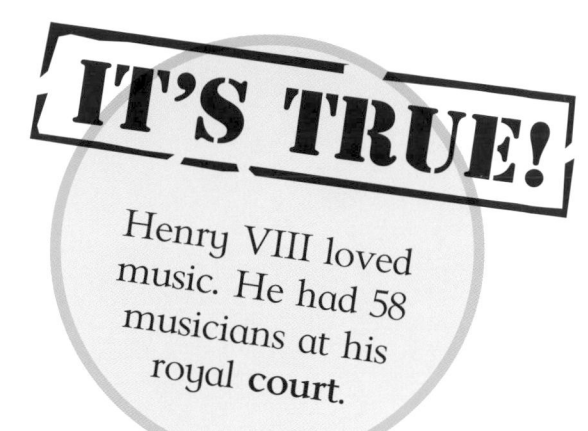

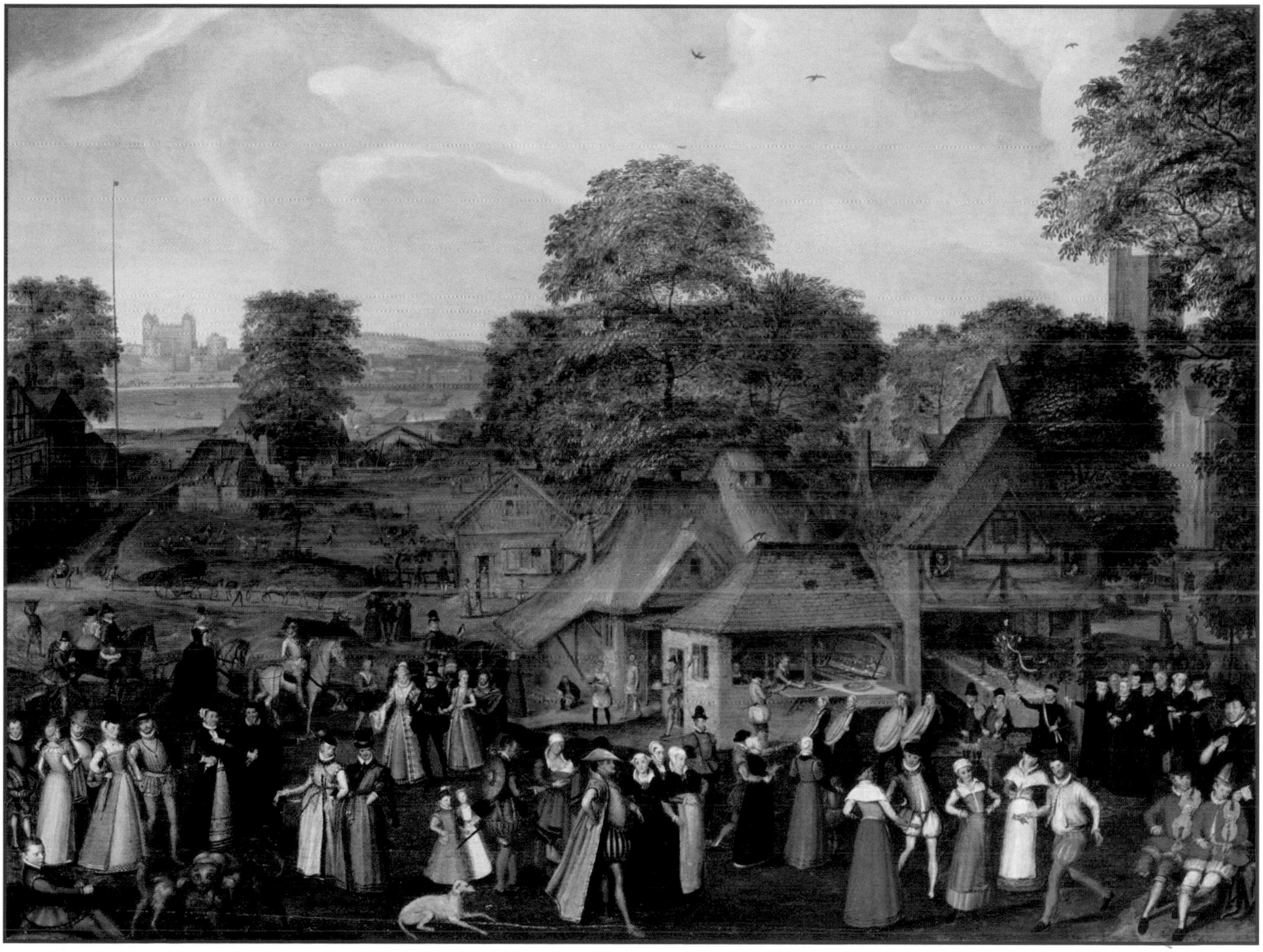

This picture from 1570 shows the grand celebrations for a wedding party in Tudor times. The beautiful clothes tell us that the wedding guests were rich.

Henry's childhood

Henry was born at Greenwich, London, in 1491. His parents were King Henry VII and Elizabeth of York. Henry never expected to be a **monarch** as his older brother Arthur was due to be king. When Arthur died, Henry was next in line to the throne.

Henry VIII became king of England in 1509. He was not yet eighteen years old.

Henry was known as the Prince of Wales. The young prince enjoyed life. He was sporty and clever. He liked to play the organ and the **lute**. He also loved to **joust**.

IT'S TRUE!

Henry played tennis when he was older. But he was so unfit that a servant threw the ball up in the air for him!

Jousting was a dangerous sport. Henry would have worn a suit of armour to protect himself like the one this model knight is wearing.

The young king

Henry VIII was crowned king in 1509, when he was just 17 years old. Weeks later, he married his brother's **widow**. Her name was Catherine of Aragon.

Catherine of Aragon came over from Spain to marry Henry's brother, Arthur. She married Henry eight years after Arthur's death.

The young king soon went to battle. England joined with Spain to fight France. Henry gave money to the Royal Navy so they could build more ships.

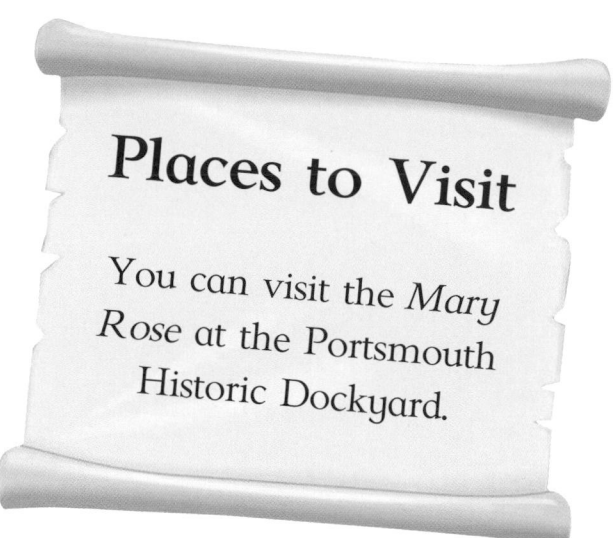

Places to Visit

You can visit the *Mary Rose* at the Portsmouth Historic Dockyard.

The *Mary Rose* was one of Henry VIII's favourite battleships. She sank in 1545, but was rescued from the seabed over four hundred years later, in 1982.

A son and heir

Henry VIII wanted a son more than anything else. This son would become king when Henry died. However, Princess Mary was the only one of Catherine's six children to live.

Henry VIII loved his daughter, Princess Mary. But he still really wanted a son and **heir**.

Henry decided to marry a woman called Anne Boleyn instead so that she might give him a son. However, Henry was still married to Catherine and the **Roman Catholic Church** didn't believe in **divorce**.

Places to Visit

Ludlow Castle is in Shropshire. Princess Mary had a **court** there when she was just nine years old. The castle is now ruined, but still spectacular.

Anne Boleyn was famous in the court of Henry VIII for her fashionable clothes. Many rich women copied the style of dresses that she wore.

Trouble with the Pope

Henry VIII and the Pope got on well. But when Henry wanted to **divorce** his wife, the Pope got angry. The **Roman Catholic Church** does not allow divorce. The king was so cross that he broke away from the Roman Catholic Church.

Although Henry VIII was King of England, Pope Clement VII refused to allow him to divorce Catherine of Aragon.

In 1533, Henry VIII formed his own church. It was called the **Church of England**. He was now able to divorce Catherine of Aragon and marry Anne Boleyn.

This picture shows Henry VIII introducing Anne Boleyn at **court**. Anne was crowned Queen in June 1553.

Henry's wives

Anne Boleyn gave Henry VIII another daughter, Elizabeth. By now, Henry was 42 and he worried that he might never have a son. He then married Jane Seymour. She gave birth to a boy, Prince Edward, but died herself soon after.

Henry VIII said his third wife, Jane Seymour, was his only 'true wife'. This is because she gave him a son and **heir**.

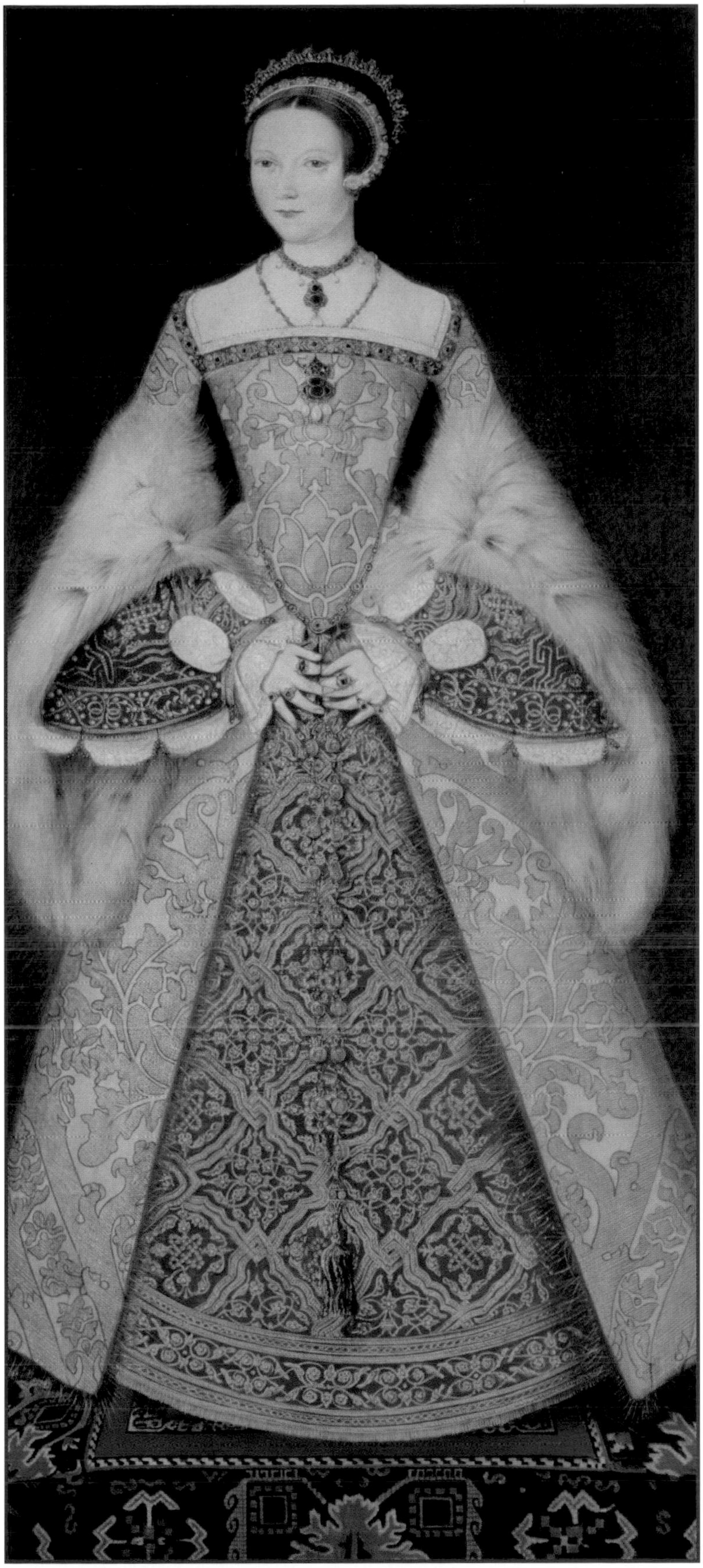

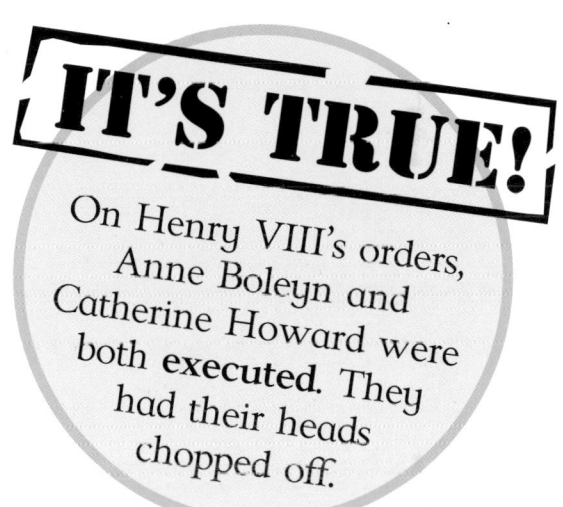

Henry married three more times. His wives were Anne of Cleves, Catherine Howard and Catherine Parr.

IT'S TRUE!

On Henry VIII's orders, Anne Boleyn and Catherine Howard were both **executed**. They had their heads chopped off.

Catherine Parr was the last of the six wives of Henry VIII. She outlived her husband by just one year.

Religious changes

Once he had split with the **Roman Catholic Church**, Henry did his best to get rid of the Catholic **religion** in his own country. He wanted everyone to join the new **Church of England**.

Sir Thomas More was an important politician. Henry VIII had him **executed** for **treason** when he refused to become a **Protestant**.

He took away the Catholics' **monasteries.** Some were destroyed. Others were sold. Many people suffered because of Henry's actions.

IT'S TRUE!

Henry's daughter Mary was a **Catholic**. When she became queen she killed so many **Protestants** she was called Bloody Mary!

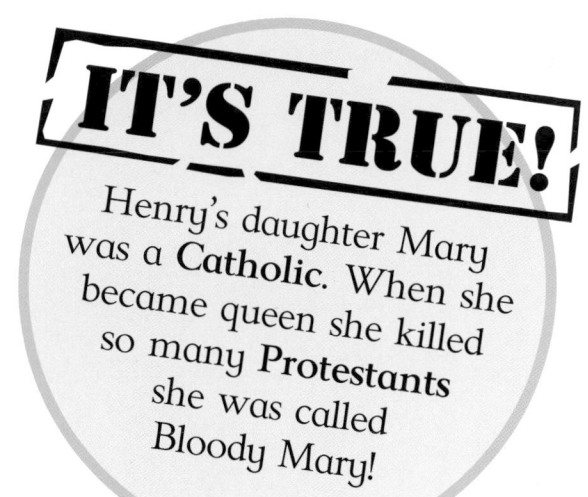

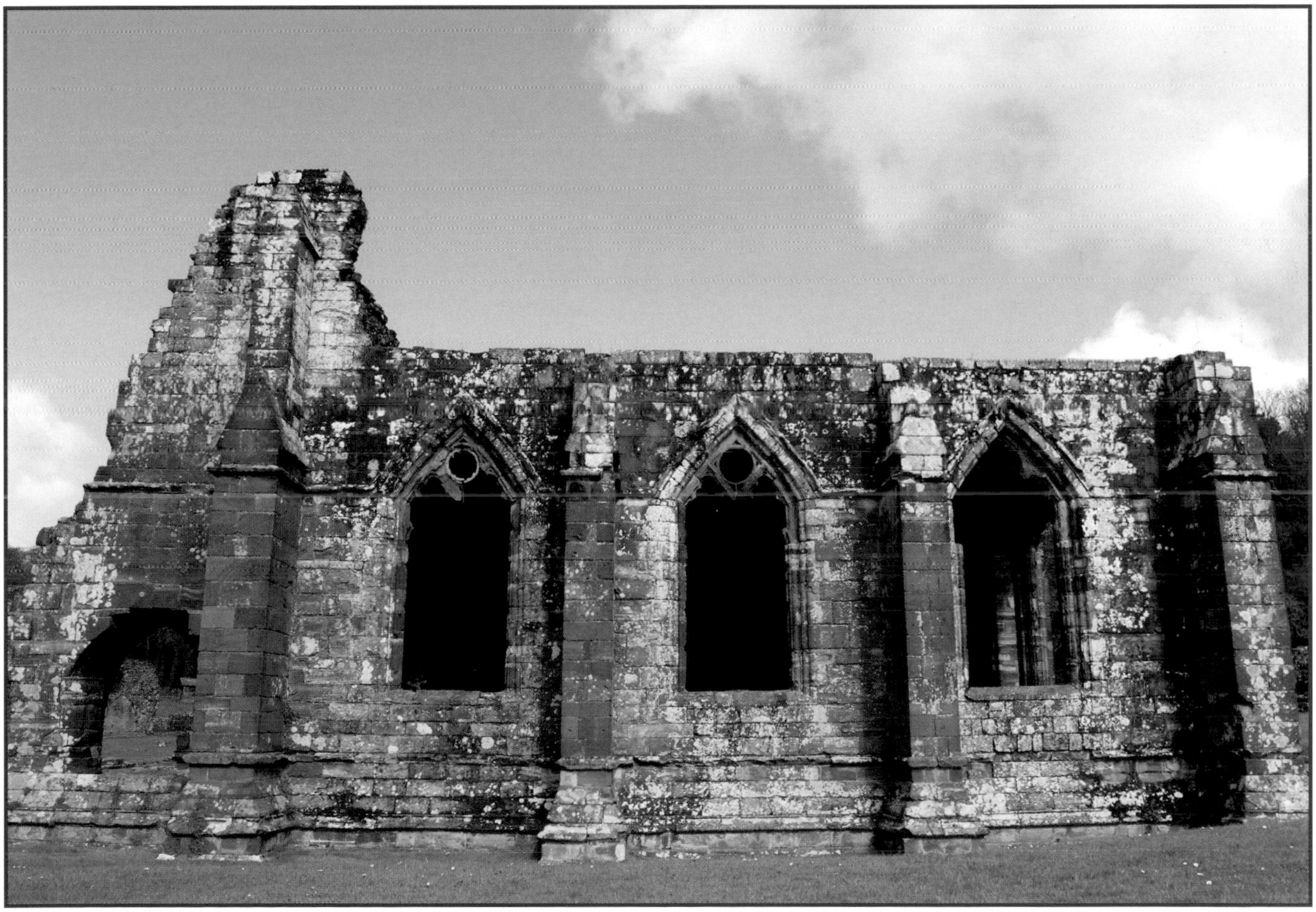

Furness Abbey in Cumbria was one of the religious buildings closed by Henry VIII. You can visit its ruins today.

The old king

Henry VIII loved to eat and drink. After he was hurt in a **jousting** accident, it was harder for him to exercise. He grew fatter and fatter. His legs were swollen and painful. He was often carried on a chair and lifted up and down stairs.

Henry VIII's waist measurement was a huge 137 cm.

King Henry VIII died at the age of 55. He was buried at Windsor Castle next to his favourite wife, Jane Seymour.

Places to Visit

Henry VIII spent much of his later life at Hampton Court Palace. His Royal Tennis Court is still used today.

Henry VIII is buried in St George's Chapel, Windsor Castle. Many other members of the royal family are also buried there.

The next monarch

Henry VIII did leave the crown to the male **heir** he so wanted. However, it wasn't to last. The young Edward VI died six years later. His elder sister came next. Mary I was queen for just five years.

Edward VI was just nine years old when he became king of England.

But one of Henry VIII's children was to be a very great **monarch** indeed. Queen Elizabeth I was his daughter by Anne Boleyn. She reigned from 1558 to 1603.

IT'S TRUE!

Elizabeth I never married and never had any children. She was the very last of the Tudor monarchs.

Elizabeth was a popular monarch who ruled for forty-five years.

Timeline

1491	Henry is born on 28 June
1509	The young king is crowned Henry VIII Marries Catherine of Aragon
1516	Henry's daughter Mary is born
1533	Henry leaves the Roman Catholic Church Henry divorces Catherine of Aragon Marries Anne Boleyn Henry's daughter Elizabeth is born
1534	Becomes Head of the Church of England
1536	Anne Boleyn is executed Marries Jane Seymour
1537	Henry's son Edward is born
1540	Marries Anne of Cleves Marries Catherine Howard
1542	Catherine Howard is executed
1543	Marries Catherine Parr
1547	Henry VIII dies on 28 January Edward VI becomes king
1553	Mary I becomes queen
1558	Elizabeth I becomes queen

Glossary

Catholics people who believe that the Pope is the head of the Roman Catholic Church

Church of England the English branch of the Western Christian Church. It has the country's monarch as its head

court a royal person's household, where they live, entertain and are looked after by servants

divorce the legal ending of a marriage

executed when someone is killed as a punishment

heir the heir to the throne becomes the next monarch of a country

joust to fight on horseback with long, pointed weapons called lances

lute a stringed instrument with a long neck, rounded body and flat front. It is a bit like a guitar

monarch the ruler of a country, such as a king or queen

monasteries houses where monks live and work

Protestants people who believe that the king or queen is the head of the Church of England

religion what people believe about God or gods, and how they worship

Roman Catholic Church the part of the Christian Church that has the Pope as its head

treason a crime against a country or its king or queen

widow a woman whose husband has died

Further information

Books

The Secret Life of Henry VIII by Bob Fawke (Hodder Children's Books, 2005)

The Tudors by Liz Gogerly (Wayland, 2005)

Usborne History of Britain: Internet-linked Tudors and Stuarts by Fiona Patchett (Usborne Publishing, 2006)

Websites

http://www.maryrose.org/dive_in/mary_rose.html

(Mary Rose at Portsmouth Historic Dockyard)

Watch an animated movie about the history of the Mary Rose

www.bbc.co.uk/schools/famouspeople/standard/henry

Play a game to help put Henry VIII's armours on

Index